ACNE

The Essential Guide

Need
— 2 —
Know

Antonia
Mariconda

D0493278

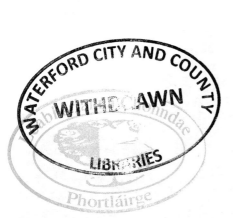

First published in Great Britain in 2009 by
Need2Know
Remus House
Coltsfoot Drive
Peterborough
PE2 9JX
Telephone 01733 898103
Fax 01733 313524
www.need2knowbooks.co.uk

Need2Know is an imprint of Forward Press Ltd.
www.forwardpress.co.uk
SB ISBN 978-1-86144-075-4
Cover photograph: StockXpert

Contents

Introduction 5

Chapter **1** What is Acne? 9

Chapter **2** Who Can Suffer From Acne? 19

Chapter **3** Diagnosing Acne 25

Chapter **4** Treatments 31

Chapter **5** Myths Dispelled 45

Chapter **6** Acne and You 49

Chapter **7** Skin Care 57

Chapter **8** Expert Advice 63

Chapter **9** Case Studies 73

Help List 79

Book List 87

Glossary 89

Introduction

Acne is the most common chronic skin condition, affecting almost all adolescents at some point in their lives. For most people, acne tends to disappear by the time they reach their mid-20s, but some may continue to experience the skin condition well into their adult life (www.netdoctor.co.uk).

Although acne is common, it can still be very distressing. Dermatologists (specialist physicians who diagnose and treat diseases of the skin) and GPs are faced with hundreds of cases every year. Dealing with acne is not always straightforward as it can cause severe scarring, not only physically but mentally as well.

Using medical research and expert advice from experienced skin professionals, this book provides a concise and detailed guide to the diagnosis, treatment and management of acne.

This book will:

- Explain in clear language exactly what acne is.

- Detail all the different types of acne.

- Explain who can suffer from acne (it is not a condition reserved just for teenagers!).

- Help you find a reliable diagnosis if you think you may have acne.

- Help you understand how acne can make you feel and point you in the direction of further support.

- Dispel many of the common myths and misconceptions.

- Guide you through the treatments available and explain how they work.

- Offer you expert advice from qualified medical dermatologists and skin professionals.

- Answer many of the frequently asked questions.

- Offer you details of organisations, helplines and websites that give advice and information.

At the back of the book is a help list detailing useful websites and organisations, a book list containing many helpful publications relating to acne and a glossary with all the medical terms clearly explained.

Acne can have a profound effect on the life of sufferers. Just as with any other condition, it can cause some people a lot of distress. However, the good news is that acne is treatable and can be managed successfully if the right advice and help is sought.

No matter how old you are, this guide will point you in the direction of suitable help and support specific to your own skin and the way you feel.

Acknowledgements

I would like to thank all of the individuals who have contributed medical information to this book, especially Dr Marco La Malfa for his patience, expert advice and guidance. I would also like to acknowledge the following:

Dr Sandeep Cliff
Shaf Khan
Jan Birch
Professor Laurence Kirwan
Dr Robin Stones
Dr Debra Luftman
Dr Cuross Bakhtiar
All the professional authorities and associations mentioned in this guide.

Disclaimer

This book is for general information about acne only. It is not intended to replace professional medical advice although it can be used alongside it. Anyone with acne, or who suspects that they have a skin condition, should seek medical advice from a healthcare professional such as their GP in the first instance.

Chapter One

What is Acne?

Our skin is the part of us we show to the world and its appearance can reflect our age, origin, health and general wellbeing. One in three people will experience some kind of skin problem during their lifetime and nearly everyone will get a spot or two at some point. Unfortunately, clinical acne can be a serious problem for some people, sometimes persisting beyond the teenage years.

Acne (also referred to formally as acne vulgaris, meaning common acne) is a skin condition that causes pimples and usually affects the skin of the face, back, neck, chest and arms. The severity of the condition can vary. About 80-90% of teenagers are affected by acne between the ages of 13 and 18. However, adults can also get acne and it is estimated that 25% of all adults are affected by the condition at any one time. This is known as late-onset acne.

Acne is one of the most widespread medical conditions in the world, but at the moment there is no known cure. However, it is managable and early intervention is essential in treating most types of acne. It is important to take action and find a treatment that works for you as the sooner the problem is addressed, the less likely it is that there will be permanent damage to your skin.

Contrary to popular belief, acne is not caused by anything you may or may not be doing. For example, the food you eat does not affect the condition of your acne. You can read more about the myths and misconceptions surrounding acne in chapter 5.

Acne is influenced by a combination of factors which are at work far beneath the surface of your skin – factors which you have no control over. Research is ongoing to improve our understanding of acne and, while there is no definitive cure, there is an impressive array of treatments to manage the condition effectively and successfully. A little dedication and patience is the key requirement.

Understanding how our skin works

To understand why acne spots develop, you first need to know a bit about the normal structure and function of human skin. How our skin works is something that many of us are not really aware of and can take for granted on a day-to-day basis.

Skin has many functions and serves us far more than just as a covering for the body. Some of these functions are so important that unless most of the skin is working efficiently, the body itself can suffer as a result.

With a surface area between 1.5m^2 and 2m^2 and weighing about 11kg for the average adult, our skin is our largest organ. Skin is also one of the seven channels of elimination (the systems by which the body eliminates waste and toxins). Containing about 70% water, 25% protein and 2% lipids (oily substances), the skin helps the main organs of elimination (liver, kidneys and intestines) get rid of waste build-up.

The function of the skin

As well as getting rid of unwanted products and giving us our appearance and shape, the skin also acts as a:

- Physical barrier. The outer layer of the skin consists of dead skin cells which are continually being shed from the surface and replaced from below. The dead skin cells form a protective layer which is also resistant to water.

- Defence against infection. Human skin is covered in bacteria, but these do not result in an active infection if they are confined to the dead outer layer. In addition, the skin contains sebaceous glands (the glands of the skin that produce oil) which, after childhood, produce a natural 'fungistatic substance' called sebum that helps protect the skin against fungal infections.

- Temperature control mechanism. Human skin is covered with hair and contains numerous blood vessels and sweat glands. If the body is in danger of becoming too cold, the hairs stand on end to produce an insulating layer and the blood vessels narrow to help prevent heat escaping through the skin. The mechanisms to prevent overheating include the blood vessels widening to encourage heat loss from the skin's surface and sweat production by the sweat glands which causes cooling by evaporation. In summary, we carry around with us a very sophisticated form of personal air conditioning!

- Sensory organ. The skin has nerve cells which respond to pressure, temperature and pain. These allow us to feel touch, sense how hot or cold something is or determine whether something hurts us or not. We can then react accordingly, potentially saving ourselves from harmful situations such as burning our hands on a hot pan!

The structure of the skin

Your skin is a complicated structure with many varied functions and from the moment you are born, it begins a lifelong process of shedding dead cells, renewing itself and producing oil. This process is affected by your hormone balance which changes throughout your life. If any of the structures in the skin are not working properly, spots, a rash or an abnormal sensation can occur.

Our skin is made up of three important parts:

- Epidermis (outer layer) – a flat layer of skin (made from about 15 individual layers of skin) that is constantly flaking off. When you exfoliate with a cream or body wash, you remove dead skin cells from this layer. The epidermis is made from cells called keratinocytes – they have this name because they produce a protein called keratin. Keratin is important as it gives the skin its strength to resist physical wear and tear and also makes the skin waterproof. The other layers of skin below the epidermis are constantly producing new cells. At the beginning of their life, these cells are square and sit at the base of the epidermis layer. Over time, their internal structure starts to break down and they become flatter. As they become flatter, they 'rise' to the surface and turn into the outer layer of skin.

- Dermis – this layer of skin gets its name from the Greek word for skin. The

'Your skin is a complicated structure with many varied functions and from the moment you are born, it begins a lifelong process of shedding dead cells, renewing itself and producing oil.'

dermis is mostly made up of collagen and elastin. Collagen is a protein naturally found in connective tissue and elastin is a protein made from thin, stretchy fibres. The dermis has two parts: the upper area, made from lots of blood vessels and nerve endings, and the lower area, made from a thick mesh of fibres. The dermis holds the hair follicles and sweat glands. The hair follicles are shafts that run the whole depth of the dermis and up through the epidermis where they appear on the surface of the skin. On the side of each hair follicle is a very small gland that produces sebum (the skin's natural oil). The pores of the skin start deep in the dermis layer and are spiral shaped sweat ducts that travel up to the surface of the skin. This layer of skin is attached to the deepest part, the subcutaneous layer.

- Subcutaneous layer – the third and bottom layer of the skin. It is made up of connective tissues and fats. This layer holds everything in place and protects and insulates the internal structure of the body.

The causes of acne

'It is absolutely essential that you do not blame yourself for your acne. The reality is that acne is caused by a combination of factors that take place far beneath your skin which, unfortunately, you have no control over.'

It is absolutely essential that you do not blame yourself for your acne. The reality is that acne is caused by a combination of factors that take place far beneath your skin which, unfortunately, you have no control over.

While acne is not curable (at the moment), it is definitely treatable. Thanks to great developments in research and medicine, we now know more about controlling the condition than ever before. The best route to managing acne is prevention: stopping the condition before it creates advanced, visual symptoms.

How it begins

An acne blemish actually starts in your hair follicles (pores) approximately two to three weeks before it appears on your skin's surface.

Deep within each follicle, your sebaceous glands work to produce sebum, the oil that keeps your skin moist and supple. If you are prone to acne, testosterone (a hormone found naturally in both men and women) triggers the sebaceous glands to produce excess sebum.

As your skin renews itself, the old cells die, mix with your skin's natural oils and come off. Under normal circumstances, these cells come off easily, making room for the new skin. However, everyone is different and some people will shed cells unevenly, causing dead cells to become sticky and clump together, eventually forming a plug which traps oil and bacteria inside the follicle.

This plug (also known as a comedone) begins to swell as your skin continues its normal production of sebum. Your body then attacks the bacteria with a host of white blood cells which culminate in a spot, appearing on the surface of your skin.

One of the best weapons in the fight against acne is knowledge. If you know what causes acne, it will be easier for you to devise a good plan of defence.

There are five primary culprits contributing to this process which leads to acne. Each of these factors can vary dramatically between individuals. While you don't have control over these factors, understanding them can help you in your search for a proper acne treatment and management plan.

The five culprits

- Hormones: for the majority of acne sufferers, the condition begins at puberty when the body starts to produce hormones called androgens. The androgen testosterone causes the sebaceous glands to enlarge, but in acne sufferers this natural process is affected and the sebaceous glands are over-stimulated. This can persist into adulthood. Androgens are also responsible for acne flare-ups associated with the menstrual cycle and occasionally pregnancy.

- Extra sebum: when the sebaceous gland is stimulated, it produces extra sebum. This sebum travels up the follicle and mixes with bacteria and dead skin cells that have been shed from the lining of the follicle. While this process is normal, the presence of extra sebum increases the chances of clogging in the follicle which can cause acne.

- Follicle fallout: normally, dead cells within the follicle shed progressively and are expelled onto the skin's surface. However, in people with overactive sebaceous glands these cells are shed more rapidly. Mixed with a surplus of sebum, the dead skin cells form a plug in the follicle, preventing the skin from renewing naturally.

- Bacteria: a bacterium called Propionibacterium acnes (P acnes for short!) is naturally present on all skin types as part of the skin's natural sebum maintenance system. However, once a follicle is plugged, P acnes bacteria multiply rapidly, creating a chemical reaction that generates inflammation in the follicle and the surrounding skin.

- Inflammation: when your body encounters these unwanted bacteria, it sends a defence force of white blood cells to attack the intruders, producing an inflammatory response in a process called chemotaxis. This causes the characteristic red, swollen and painful pimples that most people associate with acne.

Different types of acne spots

Acne can include a variety of spots, ranging in severity from mild to severe. You do not have to have all of the types listed below for you to have acne – just having one type could mean that you have the condition. The good news is that there are treatments available to address all of the spot variations listed below.

Comedones

Comedones are the starting point of all acne. They are very small blockages in the pores of your skin. Normally, at this stage they are referred to as microcomedones as they are incredibly tiny in size. Microcomedones can either progress to become larger comedones or they can burst internally and cause any of the different types of spots mentioned opposite and over the page. A microcomedone can burst because of a build up of internal pressure.

Whiteheads

A whitehead is a microcomedone that gets larger due to swelling behind the blockage, and slowly it becomes much more visible. If the initial blockage is quite deep in the pore, the opening on the skin will remain closed. This causes the typical whitish lump that can be seen and felt on the surface of the skin. Some people think of a whitehead as a type of white pus-like spot, but a whitehead is actually a closed comedone.

Blackheads

Unlike a whitehead, a blackhead is an open comedone. Blackheads are clearly visible and appear darker on the skin. The appearance of a blackhead means that the blockage occured further up the duct, widening the opening of the pore and making the contents visible. A blackhead normally has a hard plug which is a mixture of solidified sebum and dead cells that have shed. It is the skin cells which contain dark pigment called melanin and give the impression that the spot is black and not dirt as many people often suppose.

Comedones can linger within your skin for months and, sometimes, even years. They can live in your skin without changing or they may either progress or burst (rupture). As a consequence, different types of spots can result on the surface of your skin. These spots are either papules, pustules, nodules or cysts (see below).

Papules

If a comedone starts to leak sebum into the surrounding tissue, it will produce an inflammation which then produces a red spot. Papules are normally less than 5mm in width and do not have any visible pus on the surface. Instead, they have a red head. If your microcomedones rupture, your skin will produce papules. This also means that your skin would have not gone through the whitehead or blackhead stage, as it burst before it had a chance to.

Pustules

A pustule, as the word itself suggests, is a typical pus spot or yellow head. A pustule will occur when the bacteria present on your skin and within the duct starts to multiply. These bacteria, P acnes, prefer dark places with little air.

A blocked pore is ideal for these bacteria to multiply. When your body's natural defences move into action to defend themselves against the bacteria, they send an army of white blood cells to attack the intruders. This produces the inflammatory response in a process called chemotaxis and leads to a head of pus on a red swelling.

Comedones, papules and pustules are easy to see because of the inflammation and swelling they cause. They can also be quite painful in some instances. However, it may be reassuring to know that these types of spots normally clear up without causing much scarring (except sometimes in people who have darker or pigmented skin). The following two types of spots can be more aggressive and sometimes leave more significant scars.

Nodules

A nodule is a solid spot that is bigger than a papule and originates much deeper in the skin. When a large comedone ruptures it releases lots of inflammatory content such as bacteria and white cells into the surrounding skin. This causes a nodule to form which is more inflamed and contains more pus, leading to more pain and swelling. A nodule has a deeper root into the subcutaneous layer of skin (the deepest part) and it is this extended damage that can lead to scarring.

Cysts

Cysts are bags of liquid that contain a combination of bacteria and pus. Usually, cysts occur alongside nodules and can appear as a small group of two or three close together. Cysts are more aggressive than nodules and can be quite destructive to the structure of the skin. Fortunately, cysts are generally quite rare.

In simple terms...

All acne begins with the comedone which, put simply, is an enlarged hair follicle plugged (for various reasons) with dead skin cells, oil and bacteria, invisible to the naked eye. Comedones will linger beneath the surface of your skin waiting for the right conditions to grow inflamed and progress into one of the different types of spots:

- Whiteheads.
- Blackheads.
- Papules.
- Pustules.
- Nodules.
- Cysts.

'All acne begins with the comedone which, put simply, is an enlarged hair follicle plugged with dead skin cells, oil and bacteria, invisible to the naked eye.'

Summing Up

■ Acne is one of the most widespread medical conditions in the world, so you are definitely not alone.

■ Hormones, extra sebum (oil found in the skin), follicle fallout, bacteria and inflammation are the five main culprits contributing to the acne process.

■ An acne spot starts life two to three weeks beneath the surface of your skin before you actually start to see it.

■ There are several different types of spots that can be found in acne, ranging in shape, form and appearance.

Chapter Two

Who Can Suffer
From Acne?

According to the NHS, about 80-90% of people will experience acne to some degree between the ages of 13 and 18. Many of these young people are able to manage their acne with over-the-counter (non-prescription) treatments. For some, however, acne is more serious and requires treatment from a GP or dermatologist.

The website www.netdoctor.co.uk states that, for most, acne goes away by the time they are in their 20s. However, people with very sensitive skin can continue to experience the condition until they are in the 40s. In some cases, people get acne for the first time as adults.

Acne can affect men and women equally but there are differences in the type of spots they get. According to consultant dermatologist Dr Sandeep Cliff, men are more likely to have severe, longer lasting forms of acne. Despite this, men are less likely than women to visit a dermatologist for their acne. Women are more likely to have acne due to hormonal changes associated with their menstrual cycle and acne caused by cosmetics.

'According to the NHS, about 80-90% of people will experience acne to some degree between the ages of 13 and 18.'

Types of acne

Dermatologists have identified many types of acne. Some of the most common types include:

- Adolescent acne.
- Infantile acne.
- Occupational acne.

- Drug-induced acne.

- Acne caused by occlusion.

- Cosmetic-induced acne.

- Acne conglobata.

- Keloid acne.

Each type of acne can occur in people of any age, except for infantile acne which only develops in babies.

The most common type is adolescent acne. This is due to elevated hormone levels during puberty (see chapter 1 for more information on the causes of acne including the role of hormones, as well as the end of this chapter).

Adolescent acne can begin during the early teenage years and can last for around five to 10 years. In some adolescents, more severe acne follows the development of comedones, reaching a peak three to five years after the first comedones appear. Adolescent acne commonly disappears during the mid-20s. However, severe acne, also known as nodular acne or cystic acne, may not settle until later.

The other types of acne

Infantile acne

Infantile acne may be present at birth or develop in babies during the first few months of life. Children and infants can also fall prey to a type of acne called acne mechanica, caused by the prolonged use of school caps or straps on school bags.

Occupational acne

Occupational acne is caused by exposure of the skin to chemicals and other irritant substances found in the workplace.

Drug-induced acne

This is a type of acne caused as a result of taking certain types of drugs or medication.

Occlusion acne

Tight fitting garments and accessories, when worn for long periods of time, can cause acne, especially in hot or humid conditions. This type of acne is most strongly associated with those in the military services and those who engage in fetishist activities.

Cosmetic-induced acne

Cosmetic-induced acne is, as the name suggests, a type of acne caused by the use, or overuse, of certain cosmetics and skin care products.

Acne conglobata

This is one of the severest forms of acne and can lead to scarring. It is characterised by burrowing and interconnecting abscesses and irregular scars. Acne conglobata is more common in males.

Keloid acne

Keloid acne is quite severe. It is characterised by chronic bumpy spots, usually found on the face and neck. It is most commonly found in males and causes scarring.

Adult acne

There is a vast assortment of acne types that can affect adults (male or female). Adult women are especially prone to pyoderma faciale, a type of acne which can cause large painful pustules, nodules and cysts on the face.

'Cosmetic-induced acne is, as the name suggests, a type of acne caused by the use, or overuse, of certain cosmetics and skin care products.'

It can leave permanent scarring, especially on darker complexions. It most often occurs in women who have never experienced acne before and generally clears up within a year.

Adult males are more likely to suffer from acne conglobata and acne fulminans, an extreme and sudden appearance of acne conglobata accompanied by a fever and aching joints. The other general types of acne may also affect adults.

Adult acne can be broadly divided into two types: persistent acne which has continued from the teenage years into adulthood and late-onset acne which appears for the first time after the age of 25. More research is required to fully understand the causes of adult acne.

Hormones and acne

Hormones play a crucial part in the development of acne. The ones that have a major influence on acne are the sex hormones and during puberty large quantities begin to be produced. Androgens such as testosterone are the main male hormones, while progesterone and oestrogen are the main female hormones. It may sound peculiar but women actually produce male hormones too. Oestrogen is made from testosterone by special cells in the ovaries and, as not all of it is used, some passes into the blood stream and circulates around the body. It is the testosterone that causes the sebaceous glands to enlarge and become over-stimulated resulting in acne.

The female hormones can have a modifying effect on the action of the testosterone which is why hormonal changes and treatments really only apply to women. However, progesterone makes skin more sensitive to the testosterone present and as this stimulates the production of sebum, there is more of a chance of acne appearing.

Females experience hormonal changes at different points during their life which can manifest in the form of acne. This is why some females, whether adolescents or adults, can experience spots just before or during a period. This usually occurs because hormone levels during the monthly cycle change, and close to ovulation (when eggs are produced) the levels of progesterone

'Progesterone makes skin more sensitive to the testosterone present and as this stimulates the production of sebum, there is more of a chance of acne appearing.'

increase. In summary, progesterone will tend to make acne worse, while oestrogen can make it better by making the skin less responsive and sensitive to testosterone.

Another factor which can also cause acne in women is pregnancy – when the body produces higher levels of female hormones to make sure that it can support the changes needed for a healthy baby. Hormones usually return to a normal state after pregnancy ends.

Other medically-related conditions occurring in females such as polycystic ovarian syndrome can also be a factor in causing acne. This, again, is caused by a hormonal change in the body where slightly higher levels of testosterone are produced and are not changed into oestrogen efficiently. This leads to more testosterone getting into the blood stream and affecting the skin.

Summing Up

- Acne is a skin disorder which can affect everyone.

- A person of any background or age can suffer from acne, even babies!

- There are many different types of acne – the most common being adolescent acne.

- According to Margaret Stearn in her book *Warts and All: Straight Talking Advice on Life's Embarrassing Problems*, at 40 years of age, five women in every 100 and one man in every 100 suffers from acne.

Chapter Three

Diagnosing Acne

How do I know if I have acne?

If you are not sure whether you have acne, the first step is to make an appointment with your GP. It is important that you give them as much information as possible about your condition that may help in the overall assessment of your problem. The information you provide your GP with will help to make an accurate diagnosis.

Don't be afraid to tell your GP if you feel down about your condition or if it is having a social impact on you. For example, you might feel reluctant to meet new people as you are self-conscious about the condition of your skin. See chapter 6 for more information on talking to your GP about the psychological effects acne can have on you.

By giving as much information to your GP as possible, you are indicating that you are taking your condition seriously and that you expect him or her to do the same.

Questions your GP may ask you:

- How long have you had the condition?

- Have you tried any remedies, medications or over-the-counter products?

- Where have you noticed the spots occurring? Is it just the face? Are there any on your back, neck or chest?

- Do you notice that the spots become worse at certain times? Are the spots worse when you exercise, use cosmetics or feel stressed?

'The information you provide your GP with will help to make an accurate diagnosis.'

Once you have explained all aspects of your condition, your GP will check your medical history. This will include questions about your skin, diet and any medication you regularly take. A visual inspection is then carried out.

This visual inspection will determine whether the symptoms you have are acne or not. Your GP will carry out a physical examination of the face, upper neck, chest, shoulders and back, as these are the areas most often affected by acne. The doctor determines the number and type of blemishes, whether they are inflamed or not, whether they are deep or near the surface of the skin and whether there is scarring or skin discolouration.

From a visual inspection, your GP should be able to tell which grade of acne you have. The grade determines how severe your acne is and what type of spots are present. The treatment of your acne and what ingredients will be used also depend on its grade. For more information on the ingredients mentioned below, see chapter 4.

Grade 1

Grade 1 acne is the mildest form. There may be minor spots but they will be small and appear only very occasionally in small numbers (one or two). Blackheads and milia (small white spots) will be found, sometimes in great numbers, but there is no inflammation.

Grade 1 acne is commonly seen in early adolescence, especially on the nose and/or forehead. Many adults also experience grade 1 acne as blackheads on the nose and forehead. Milia are commonly found on the eye area and chin.

This type of acne can be successfully treated at home using an over-the-counter product containing salicylic acid – see your GP for advice on which over-the-counter products would be the most effective for your skin. Results are generally seen quickly – treating acne while it is still in its early stages helps prevent it from progressing, especially in teens. Grade 1 acne may progress to grade 2 if left untreated.

Grade 2

Grade 2 is considered to be moderate. There will be blackheads and milia, generally in greater numbers. You will start seeing more papules and the formation of pustules. They will appear with greater frequency and the general breakout activity will be more visible. There will also be slight inflammation of the skin.

Adolescents may see the acne progress from the nose and forehead to other areas of the face. Acne may start to affect the chest and shoulders, with occasional breakouts on the back, especially in males. Adult women may find greater breakout activity in the cheeks, chin and jaw line area, especially just before menstruation and at other times during the menstrual cycle.

Grade 2 acne can still be treated at home using over-the-counter products. In addition to salicylic acid, a benzoyl peroxide lotion should be used daily to help kill the bacteria that cause inflamed breakouts. However, if after several weeks of home treatment your acne does not significantly improve, it is time to see a dermatologist. Grade 2 acne may progress to grade 3, especially if pimples are habitually picked at or squeezed.

Grade 3

This type of acne is considered severe. The main difference between grade 2 and 3 is the amount of inflammation present. The skin is now much more visibly reddened and inflamed. Papules and pustules have developed in greater numbers and nodules will be present.

Grade 3 usually involves other body areas such as the neck, chest, shoulders and/or upper back, as well as the face. The chance of scarring becomes higher as the infection spreads and becomes deeper.

A dermatologist should treat acne at this stage. Grade 3 acne is usually treated with both topical (creams) and systemic therapies (oral medication) available only by prescription. Left untreated, grade 3 acne may progress to grade 4.

'From a visual inspection, your GP should be able to tell which grade of acne you have. The grade determines how severe your acne is and what type of spots are present.'

Grade 4

Often referred to as nodulocystic or cystic acne, grade 4 is the most serious form of acne. The skin will display numerous papules, pustules and nodules, in addition to cysts. There is a pronounced amount of inflammation and breakouts are severe. Cystic acne is very painful.

Acne of this severity usually extends beyond the face and may affect the entire back, chest, shoulders and upper arms. The infection is deep and widespread. Nearly all cystic acne sufferers develop scarring.

Grade 4 acne must be treated by a dermatologist. It tends to be hard to control and almost always requires powerful systemic medications.

What happens next?

'You must follow your GP's advice carefully and if you are unsure about anything, ask them for more information.'

Once your GP has made a diagnosis of your acne, they may prescribe you some medication. This should begin to clear or control the severity of your acne.

You must follow your GP's advice carefully and if you are unsure about anything, ask them for more information. You should also ask if there are any side effects you can expect to experience and how long the treatment will last. Your GP may also indicate when you can start to notice an improvement in the condition of your skin.

Be sure to book a follow-up appointment with your GP as in this time you should have noticed an improvement. If you have not, you can ask what other treatments you can try. You should normally allow four to six weeks after the inital consultation to allow any medication to take affect. This period of time will also allow you to give sufficient feedback about any side effects or observations you have noticed. Be aware that results may not come quickly and that you should be prepared to pursue different avenues. Sometimes the first treatment is not always the most suitable.

It might take some time to find the right treatment for you. Patience is required as this will give your medication a chance to work properly. If you are still in doubt, you should contact your GP and explain your concerns.

Acne lookalikes

Some skin conditions can look remarkably similar to acne although their causes and treatments are different.

If you are unsure about what your skin condition is, you should consult your GP. Common skin conditions that can be mistaken for acne include:

- Rosacea – red, flushed skin with papules and pustules, especially in the nose and cheek area.

- Folliculitis – bumps or pustules caused by inflammation of the hair follicle.

- Keratosis pilaris – small, rough 'goose flesh' bumps most often found on the upper arms, thighs and buttocks and sometimes the face.

- Milaria rubra – small red bumps on the surface of the skin caused by excessive heat exposure (also referred to as heat rash).

Options available for testing and diagnosis

Many medical conditions require a blood test or urine sample for a diagnosis. However, an accurate acne diagnosis is made only with a visual examination by a GP or dermatologist.

Laboratory tests are not usually carried out unless the patient appears to have a hormonal disorder. In that case, blood tests and other tests may be ordered. These blood tests will be able to detect hormonal conditions that can cause acne such as polycystic ovarian syndrome.

Summing Up

■ Make an appointment with your GP to get a proper diagnosis.

■ Don't be tempted to rush into buying over-the-counter acne remedies before you see your GP.

■ Give your GP as much information as you can. This will ensure you get the best course of treatment for your acne. Ask your GP questions about your treatment and when you should start to see an improvement.

■ A simple visual inspection will be carried out to determine whether or not you have acne.

■ Always follow professional advice.

■ Sometimes your acne treatment may not be successful and you may have to try another one. Try to be patient as treatments can take some time to work.

'An accurate acne diagnosis is made only with a visual examination by a GP or dermatologist.'

Chapter Four

Treatments

Acne can affect different people in different ways. Some may only experience a few spots here and there while others find themselves dealing with severe outbreaks. However acne affects you, it is very likely that you are looking for a way to improve the condition of your skin.

Acne treatments do take time to start working, so it is essential that you are patient and willing to persevere.

Most treatments now available are not guaranteed to completely cure acne but they are very effective at stopping some of the problems. It is important to remember that acne can cause scarring in some cases, so you should be realistic in your expectations of the treatment.

Treatment of acne is designed to:

- Cut down the length of time you have acne.

- Reduce the swelling and inflammation in the skin which can minimise (and in some cases prevent) scarring.

- Help you feel better and reduce the psychological impact that acne may have on you.

When you first visit your GP, it is very important that you discuss how you feel your acne is affecting your work, school or social life. It is essential that your GP understands how you are feeling inside so that they can offer you the correct advice and treatment. There are many alternative therapies explained later in this chapter which could help you feel better psychologically.

The information you give your GP will help them determine which kind of treatments will work for you.

'However acne affects you, it is very likely that you are looking for a way to improve the condition of your skin.'

How your acne is treated will depend on which grade it has been diagnosed as:

- Mild acne – your GP will normally give you a treatment that you apply to the skin. This is called a topical treatment.

- Moderate acne – your GP will normally give you a topical treatment or two, perhaps combined with an oral treatment.

- Severe acne – your GP will possibly give you a topical treatment or two, perhaps combined with an oral treatment. However, your GP may also refer you to a dermatologist.

- Very severe acne – your GP will refer you to a dermatologist straightaway, while possibly also giving you a treatment.

Understanding the different types of treatments

The two following types of treatments were just mentioned above.

- Topical – medication applied directly to your skin's surface such as creams, lotions and gels.

- Oral – tablets or pills which you swallow.

It is important for your GP to make a visual diagnosis of your skin before giving you a prescription. This will ensure that the most suitable medication is given.

If you think you have only very mild acne, remember it is important that you see your GP before you start to self-manage your spots. Do not be tempted to buy over-the-counter products in a pharmacy or store without seeking professional advice. You may not be selecting the right product for your condition.

Acne treatments, whether topical or oral, do take time, so be patient. Don't expect to dab a blob of cream onto a spot and for it to disappear overnight. Having unrealistic expectations will only set you up for disappointment.

A guide to standard topical treatments

- Do consult your GP or pharmacist before purchasing any treatments to ensure that what you are applying is suitable for your type of acne. Be sure to explain your condition in as much detail as possible so he or she gives you the best advice possible.

- Do apply any topical creams sparingly to all areas affected by spots. Topical creams also work below the surface to prevent new spots from forming.

- Don't think that applying more topical treatment will help your acne clear up faster. If you do this, you could stimulate a reaction in your skin and make it more inflamed or sore.

- Do continue to wear make-up on top of acne topical treatments if you want to, but do make sure that it is oil free. Alternatively, look for cosmetic products or make-up that is described as non-comedogenic. Also be aware that during the course of some topical treatments your skin may become dry and flaky, so some creamy, liquid foundations and make-up may appear obvious. Choose light mineral make-up powders to match your skin tone.

- Don't apply topical treatments to your skin without cleaning your face first and ensuring it is free of make-up, especially at night. Topical treatments should always be applied to cleansed skin.

The key ingredients in standard topical treatments

Benzoyl peroxide

As the name suggests, benzoyl peroxide contains bleach. This works by releasing oxygen into the ducts and killing the bacteria that cause acne. It is a useful ingredient for lowering the levels of bacteria on the skin and in pores.

Azelaic acid

This preparation also comes in a cream form and acts very much in a similar way to benzoyl peroxide, though it seems to be less of an irritant. It can be obtained only through a prescription from your GP. Azelaic acid has the potential to reduce the dark pigmentation that can sometimes appear on the skin after acne has cleared up.

Nicotinamide

'Acne treatments, whether topical or oral, do take time, so be patient...Having unrealistic expectations will only set you up for disappointment.'

Nicotinamide is derived from B vitamins and helps to fight bacteria while calming the skin at the same time. To obtain this you must ask your GP for a prescription or order from a specialist chemist.

Antibiotics

There are two main topical antibiotic creams available to combat acne: erythromycin and clindamycin. They come in lotions and gels, as well as creams, which can be applied to all areas affected by acne. They are sometimes combined with other treatments such as benzoyl peroxide, zinc and also retinoid (see below).

Retinoids

Retinoids are substances that are either derived from vitamin A or are made from a synthetic type of vitamin A. Retinoids act to prevent the formation of comedones and help to remove the tiny blockages in the pores. Retinoids are also used in combination with benzoyl peroxide and antibiotics if necessary. Retinoids can also be found in tablet form but this is usually only from hospital doctors or dermatologists. The use of retinoids needs to be monitored because of potential side effects such as skin irritation, a sensitivity to sunlight, dry skin and soft internal surfaces (known as mucous membranes, found in places such as the lips, eyelids and vagina), hair loss, rashes and a thinning of the skin.

A guide to standard oral treatments

The early stage of acne spots responds well to topical treatments. For example, when pores start to become blocked, creams, lotions and gels work well.

When the skin starts to become inflamed, antibiotic treatments taken orally can help to reduce the swelling. Retinoids can then be taken to prevent further blockages. So it would be no surprise if your GP prescribed a combination of two ingredients or more in the form of topical and oral treatments. This combination can help to increase the prospect of your acne clearing up faster and more effectively.

Remember, results will not happen overnight, so be realistic in your expectations. Patience is the key to successful acne management.

- Do read the instructions of your medication carefully and make sure you understand them. If you do not use your medication properly, the chances of your treatment being fully effective are reduced.

- Do consider that your acne care should be something you do as part of a routine, just like brushing your teeth twice a day. Put in the effort and achieve the results!

- Don't take any oral treatments for acne without first consulting your GP or a pharmacist.

- Do go back to your GP for a consultation if your course of treatment has finished but your acne has returned. You may need to take antibiotics again and for a longer period of time. You may also be referred to a dermatologist.

- Don't take more than the stated dose of your tablets in the hope that the more you take, the quicker the results. This can be extremely dangerous.

- Do be aware that during the course of some oral antibiotic treatments, a few problems can occur. These can include candida (thrush) infections as the body's good bacteria are disturbed during oral antibiotic treatment. In some cases, the antibiotics can interfere with the effectiveness of certain contraceptive pills during the first weeks of a course. Ask your GP what side effects you can expect and how you should address them if they do occur.

Types of standard oral treatments

Antibiotics

Antibiotics are the main form of tablet treatment for acne. Several different types of antibiotic tablets are available, so if one type does not work, you can always try another. Your GP will explain how you should take oral antibiotics and, as with all medications, it is important you follow the instructions carefully. It is not uncommon for antibiotic tablets to be taken in combination with a topical treatment.

Hormone tablet treatments

A hormone tablet treatment is designed to help reduce the effect of male hormones present in a female. The male hormones can cause oiliness to the skin which is a main cause of acne spots. A hormone tablet called Dianette is given to females only and is the trade name of a drug called co-cyprindiol. While taking this medication, women should not become pregnant as it can damage the foetus. Dianette also contains oestrogen which means that it is a contraceptive tablet as well as an anti-acne treatment, so regular check-ups are recommended during the course. Even if you do not require contraception, Dianette is still prescribed for treating acne.

Specialist treatments

When standard treatments do not work, specialist treatments are available. If your GP refers you to a dermatologist, you may have to wait a while before you can actually see them due to an unfortunate shortage of specialists in the UK.

Do I need to see a specialist?

The following reasons could signify that you may need to see a specialist:

- You have very severe acne. The most serious form of acne, grade 4 (see chapter 3) is often referred to as nodulocystic or cystic acne. The skin will display numerous papules, pustules and nodules, in addition to cysts. There is pronounced inflammation, and breakouts are severe. Cystic acne is very painful. Acne of this severity usually extends beyond the face, affecting the entire back, chest and shoulders.

- There has been little or no response to antibiotic treatment for your acne.

- You have experienced the return of what seems to be more severe acne after a successful course of antibiotics.

- Your acne is causing you to experience severe psychological problems, such as depression or low self-esteem.

- You have noticed scarring on your skin.

Dermatologists are specialists in acne and have much more experience in using acne treatments than most GPs. They are able to prescribe more powerful treatments, such as isotretinoin.

'Dermatologists are specialists in acne and have much more experience in using acne treatments than most GPs.'

What is isotretinoin?

There is much talk in the media about the wonders of isotretinoin (brand name Roaccutane). Many people hail it as a 'cure' for acne. However, isotretinoin may not work for everybody. Isotretinoin is used to treat severe acne that is resistant to more conservative treatments such as creams and topical or oral antibiotics. Complete remission or prolonged improvement is seen in many patients after one course of isotretinoin lasting 15-20 weeks. Because of its serious side effects, isotretinoin should be used only for severe, resistant acne.

Isotretinoin works by blocking the excess sebum that clogs pores, eventually leading to acne. Many people taking this drug will not need any more treatment afterwards, but no medication is guaranteed to work effectively in all cases.

Isotretinoin is a retinoid in tablet form (they are also available as a topical cream, see page 34). Before starting you on a course of isotretinoin, your GP will ask for some blood tests. They will also require a blood test during treatment. This is because such a test is a requirement of the license to use the drug. Due to the possible side effects, the blood tests are a way of monitoring your health and ensuring that you are not developing any sensitivity or health problems as a result of the treatment.

In the UK, isotretinoin is only available through dermatologists.

A word of caution: do not buy it over the Internet. Taking isotretinoin in the wrong way could cause you harm. It is also an expensive treatment, with an average course costing £400-500.

'Isotretinoin is a strong medication that works well in many cases.'

Because of the side effects caused by isotretinoin, it is not usually prescribed for mild acne. Some of the common side effects can include extreme dryness of the skin and mucous membranes. In some cases, joint and muscle pains have been reported. Some people also report a worsening of acne during the initial period of the course, and this can cause alarm if you have not been forewarned.

If a dermatologist decides that you should take isotretinoin, you should be aware that the average course lasts approximately four months. The daily dose is normally 1mg per kilogram of your weight, but sometimes a lower dose may be given as it will prevent the initial 'worsening effect'. A whole course includes the reduced initial lower dosage and could last up to six months.

Summary of isotretinoin

Many people are afraid of isotretinoin because they believe the drug can cause depression or that they will become suicidal after using it. These are both rare side effects. Your dermatologist will monitor you to make sure you're an appropriate candidate for the medication.

Isotretinoin is a strong medication that works well in many cases. Often in medicine, the best drugs have the most side effects. Side effects for this drug are modest and easily managed by monthly visits and medical supervision.

Maintaining a low fat diet and abstaining from alcohol will usually help prevent these problems. Other less common side effects should be fully discussed with your dermatologist.

(Information courtesy of Dr Robert Sarro, Boca Raton Community Hospital, Dermatologist Associates of the Palm Beaches, USA.)

Complementary and alternative treatments

Many people suffering from acne will seek help in the form of alternative treatments and complementary medicine (also called holistic or natural medicine). Such therapies are used in addition to conventional treatment primarily to manage, prevent or reduce related side effects. They may also reduce stress and anxiety and promote healing. Complementary medicine can sit alongside traditional treatments quite well, hence the term complementary.

A whole range of different approaches to helping you manage and treat acne are available outside traditional medical treatment. The problem which is often debated where complementary or alternative treatments are concerned is the lack of scientific study that provides evidence based on results. There is little government regulation of exaggerated claims that are made by some complementary or alternative practitioners, so tread carefully when seeking either form of treatment.

Treatments like reflexology and aromatherapy may not carry a lot of scientific study which proves success, but they are treatments that certainly make you feel more relaxed and leave you feeling confident. They can ease anxiety and stress and, to some degree, raise morale – all of which is good at helping you combat the side effects of acne.

Popular complementary and alternative treatments

- Aromatherapy.
- Reflexology.
- Hypnotherapy.
- Hypnosis.

- Homeopathy.
- Autogenic training.
- Herbal treatment.
- Nutritional therapy.

Aromatherapy

Essential oils are distilled from plants and massaged over the body, mixed in a warm bath or inhaled. Once the oils enter the bloodstream, they act to produce relaxing effects. This not only improves physical health, it also affects your mood by relieving stress.

Reflexology

Reflexology suggests that the entire body is 'mapped' on the feet and hands and by applying pressure to the correct area on them, your physical health can be improved and pain removed from the afflicted body part.

Hypnotherapy

Using hypnosis to suggest positive life changes to a person is known as hypnotherapy. The patient's mind is effectively 'reprogrammed' to, for example, overcome phobias or cravings for certain foods. It can also affect your self image and reduce the signs of tension such as excessive sweating.

Hypnosis

Hypnosis is a heightened state of suggestibility. Patients are not actually unconscious – they are extremely relaxed while being focused on a dominant idea. The hypnotist can make 'suggestions' to the patient which they then implement upon 'waking' from their state of relaxation.

Homeopathy

Patients are given tablets or pills which contain highly diluted substances derived from plants, minerals and animals. The idea is to cure an illness by using a similar substance to trigger the body's natural healing process. For example, coffea (derived from coffee) can be used to cure insomnia.

Autogenic training

Autogenic training is a relaxation technique which involves the visualisation of a set of instructions, such as 'my left arm is warm and heavy'. These instructions are repeated throughout the day while sitting or lying in a relaxed position and are designed to reduce stress as well as combat anxiety and phobias.

Herbal treatment

Herbal remedies are ancient and used worldwide. Roots, leaves, seeds, flowers or stems of plants are used to treat illness, prevent disease or simply improve health. Remedies differ according to region and are used to treat conditions such as acne, depression, hair loss and even difficult pregnancies.

Nutritional therapy

Nutritional therapy seeks to cure illnesses by improving eating habits. Typically, a patient profile is constructed including past illnesses and current eating habits. A unique dietary course is then suggested.

'If you are seeking complementary therapies and treatments, do your research and consult a registered professional.'

Finding a practitioner

What you should be sure to do when finding a practitioner:

- Ask to see qualifications and evidence of training.

- Ask if they are registered with any recognised medical associates or organisations that have a code of practice. Can you have a contact number to check their membership?

- Check that the therapy the practitioner is offering is available on the NHS.

- Ensure that your practitioner is willing to keep your GP informed of the treatment they are offering.

- Check that the treatment is confidential with official records of you and your course.

- Ask for the full cost of the treatment and how long it will last.

- Ask if there are any patients who can give a testimonial of the practitioner's service.

- Make sure you are happy with the responses the practitioner gives you.

- Make sure you have information to take away with you and read at your leisure.

- Don't feel pressured into making a decision.

- Don't feel influenced by exaggerated claims to cure skin diseases.

- Be apprehensive of any practitioner who tells you to stop taking conventional treatments without consulting your GP.

Summing Up

■ Before starting any course of treatment, it is advisable to contact your GP for advice.

■ If your acne cannot be treated with standard oral or topical treatments, your GP will refer you to a specialist called a dermatologist.

■ Powerful medications available to treat acne must only be obtained through a consultant dermatologist.

■ Do not purchase medications or treatments over the Internet – it is potentially dangerous as the drugs could make your condition worse.

■ Always consult your GP before you start to use any over-the-counter remedies or treatments you have purchased.

■ If you are seeking complementary therapies and treatments, do your research and consult a registered professional.

Chapter Five

Myths Dispelled

As with many medical conditions, there are lots of myths surrounding acne and its treatment. With so much misinformation available on the Internet and by word-of-mouth, what are you supposed to listen to and how are you meant to correctly treat your acne? As well as advice from your GP, this chapter includes some accurate information for you to follow.

Myth: acne is caused by dirt

Dirt does not cause acne. Your skin is regularly dirtying and cleaning itself, shedding dead cells and then producing its own oil to nourish and hydrate the skin. It is when these natural processes fall off-balance that pores can clog and the acne cycle can begin. Rather than avoiding dirt, avoid over-washing or stripping your skin's natural oils with face washes made with alcohol. This just causes more imbalances and can actually make blemishes worse.

Myth: acne is caused by certain foods

Food is not one of the causes of acne. Chocolate, chips or pizza, along with countless other foods which have been blamed, do not cause acne. Scientists have never found a connection between diet and acne. However, eating healthy food provides essential vitamins and minerals that nourish your skin just as they do the rest of your body. Don't be afraid to indulge every now and then, but generally stick to a sensible healthy diet. For easy-to-follow recipes and healthy eating tips, see *Student Cookbook – Healthy Eating* (Need2Know).

'It is common to seek treatment early to avoid acne progression, but do not listen to hearsay – listen to facts.'

Dr Sandeep Cliff – consultant dermatologist.

Myth: only teenagers get acne

Anyone can get acne, even babies and adults. There are many different types of acne and people can develop spots for different reasons. Although it is common for teenagers to get acne, some people experience the condition for the first time as adults. Don't be afraid to seek out treatment, whatever your age.

Myth: sun tanning helps clear acne

'Anyone can get acne, even babies and adults. There are many different types of acne and people can develop spots for different reasons.'

Small amounts of sun exposure may initially improve acne by drying the skin, but it can also drain natural oil and moisture, throwing the skin further out of balance. Continuous sunbathing often increases plugging of the pores, producing blackheads, whiteheads and small pimples. The sun is many things, but it is not an effective acne cure. The fact of the matter is, the risks of sun exposure outweigh its minimal acne and oil-drying benefits. For that reason, those with acne-prone skin should always be careful in the sun. Always use a non-comedonegenic sunscreen.

Myth: acne is curable

Although there have been many significant advances in science and medicine, it is important for you to understand that there is no known definitive cure for acne yet. That is why it is crucial for you to consult your GP if you think you have the condition. Your GP, and possibly a dermatologist, will work hard to treat and manage your acne using the impressive selection of medicines, creams and pills available today.

Myth: you have to let acne run its course

Acne is a treatable condition. There is no need to wait for acne to clear up on its own. The longer you wait, the more likely your chances are of having permanent scars. If your treatment isn't working, go back to your GP.

Myth: masturbation causes acne

There is no direct link between masturbating (or any other sexual activity) and acne. Be sure to take a shower after you have been sweating as the water in sweat can cause your follicles to swell and become blocked.

Myth: acne is contagious

Acne is not contagious. However, try to avoid sharing towels with other people as acne skin is greasier and some spots can leak. It is not pleasant to share towels for hygiene reasons more than anything else.

Myth: popping spots makes them go away faster

Although popping a spot may make it seem less noticeable temporarily, it can actually cause it to stay around longer. Popping a spot pushes bacteria further into the skin, making the skin red and inflamed. Avoid the temptation if you can.

'Do not squeeze, pop or burst spots. By doing so, you create pressure that can spread the infection.'

Myth: stress causes acne

Stress may have an effect on hormones, so can theoretically promote acne. However, an effective acne treatment is more powerful at combating spots than a bout of stress is at causing them! Your time is better spent determining the right course of acne treatment rather than worrying or becoming stressed.

Myth: make-up makes acne worse

It is okay to wear make-up over prescription creams and lotions used to treat acne, but it is best to use foundation or powder which is oil free and mineral based. Be sure to thoroughly remove any make-up each night as part of your skin care routine.

Summing Up

- Do not squeeze, pop or burst spots. By doing so, you create pressure that can spread the infection.

- Take a shower after you've been sweating and/or exercising. The water in sweat causes the follicle to swell, leading the pore to become blocked and inflamed and blemishes can form.

- Drink lots of water. Water helps to flush out impurities or things that can harm your skin. It also keeps your skin hydrated and healthy.

Chapter Six

Acne and You

Dealing with the psychological scars

Acne is a not just a skin condition that causes physical changes like scars; it is also a condition that can cause emotional problems for those suffering from it.

There are now many ways of dealing with acne successfully, or at least significantly diminishing the condition. The physical aspect of acne is the most obvious, but that is not the main element in dealing with it.

Solving the emotional issues people can face when they are dealing with acne is a main part of treatment. People are affected differently by acne: some may not feel any different, whereas others can suffer mentally and socially to a great extent. There is no right or wrong way to react to your condition.

Some of the most challenging psychological effects of acne can include:

- A feeling of lowered self-esteem.

- Social withdrawal.

- A reduction in self-confidence.

- Feelings of depression.

- Feelings of anger and aggression.

- Feelings of despair.

Positive action

Collectively, the number of people who suffer from acne is very large, so you can take comfort from the fact that you are not alone. You are not 'different' or anything else you may think on a bad day. There is no need to be embarrassed by acne as it is manageable and there are people out there ready to help.

Dealing with acne can certainly be tough, but successfully overcoming its psychological and social impact comes down to your attitude and perspective on it. It is very important that you don't define yourself by your skin condition. Remember, although it might not seem like it some days, acne is not the most important thing in the world and you can take action to help yourself.

'People are affected differently by acne: some may not feel any different, whereas others can suffer mentally and socially to a great extent. There is no right or wrong way to react to your condition.'

Three key factors to recovery

Acknowledgement

The best way to deal with acne quickly and effectively is by acknowledging the problem and speaking to your GP. Be sure to explain how the condition is affecting your life and ensure you put across the seriousness of the issue. This first and crucial step can give you a huge emotional lift and will help you feel as though you are making a change for yourself.

Acceptance

Recovery from the emotional issues starts with an acceptance that there is more to acne than the simple physical scars. Speak to someone today about how you feel inside, whether that person is your GP, a member of a professional acne association or simply someone in your family.

Action

Both the physical and the emotional side of acne can now be very effectively treated as long as you are willing to take some action and act on the advice you are given. A positive mental attitude and a little patience will put you on the right track to recovery.

The 'feel good' list

If you are starting to feel really fed up with your acne, take a look at the following list. It is designed to help you feel good when you're having a bad day!

- Acne does not mean that you are dirty, unhealthy or have bad hygiene. It can happen to anyone!

- Most of us get acne when we are teenagers and nearly every teenager has experienced spots to some degree.

- Many celebrities who we perceive to be 'perfect' have had acne.

- Your acne will get better!

- Squeezing your spots will not make them go away – it could even cause scarring. Try to avoid the temptation and feel happy in the fact that you are doing the best thing by leaving them alone.

- Acne does not make you any less of a beautiful person.

- Looking in the nearest mirror every minute of the day will not make your acne go away faster! Try to focus on more important things in your life and don't let it hold you back.

- Keep yourself busy and you will soon find that you are thinking less about acne and more about the important things in life!

- Everyone else is so concerned about how they look, they don't have time to think about what you look like, let alone the condition of your skin! So hold your head high and avoid paranoia.

- Join an online forum such as the one on www.acne.org to speak to people in the same situation as you. You could also talk to friends and family that may have been through similar experiences.

'Acne does not make you any less of a beautiful person.'

▪ Do not suffer in silence. If you start to feel really down about acne and your skin, go and see your GP who will be more than happy to get you the help and support you deserve.

Dealing with the physical scars

As well as the emotional scars some people suffer as a consequence of acne, there can be many unfortunate sufferers who also experience the physical scars too. Acne can damage important structures in the skin. Certain marks (often regarded as scars as well) can improve with time, these 'scars' are called macules and they appear as red, flat marks where the acne spots used to be. They are often the last sign of inflammation in the skin and they can linger around for up to six months. Another scar or mark is the brown discolouration where the acne used to be and this is called post inflammatory hyper pigmentation, this is a result of the inflammatory process stimulating the pigment in the skin. It is quite common in darker skin and can last around 18 months.

Real scars are much longer lasting and are a result of the damage caused by the acne to the skin. Some people will scar much more easily than others, it is not an easy process to understand but it is a common occurrence in acne suffers who have nodules and cysts.

Scars tend to fall into two categories:

Extra skin tissue (raised scars)

These are called keloid or hypertrophic scars (meaning enlargement or overgrowth). These kind of scars vary from 1mm-1cm in size (sometimes bigger). The scars tend to last for years but in some cases will flatten off and shrink in size.

Loss of skin tissue (sunken scars)

These are much more common than raised scars and show up as pits in the skin. There are several types of sunken scars:

- Depressed scars – these have sharp edges and steep sides and the base of them is firm to the touch. They are generally quite large.

- Ice pick scars – these resemble wounds from an ice pick, with jagged edges and steep sides, commonly found on cheeks.

- Soft scars – the skin within these scars is quite shallow and thin. They are usually found on the face but can also appear on the body and can be up to 1cm or more.

- Follicular macular atrophy (small atrophic patches) – these scars are most likely to appear on the chest and back after extensive acne. Where the skin is damaged, the skin bulges up into soft little lumps that often look like whiteheads. They can take months or years to improve as the skin takes time to repair the damage.

Treating scars

It is wise to spend some time talking to medical professionals about the treatment of scars. You will need to get some realistic answers about what treatments are available and what results can be achieved.

Talk to your GP or dermatologist – sometimes in extreme cases your GP may refer you to a plastic surgeon. Before committing to a treatment for acne scars, ensure you have had all your questions answered by a professional. A GP, dermatologist or a plastic surgeon would need to conduct a full examination and determine whether treatment can, or should, be undertaken.

There are many different treatments available now for acne scars including chemical peels and laser and dermabrasion treatments.

Achieving a good result is something that only a professional will be able to discuss with you. You need to be realistic in your expectations as scars can't always be completely removed.

Treating the scars you have as a result of acne should not just be about the physical improvements but the psychological improvements too. Perhaps a course of counselling would help you to manage your expectations about the procedure you have chosen, as well as aid the healing process and your thoughts and feelings about the future.

The objective of scar treatment is to give the skin a more 'acceptable' physical appearance. Total restoration of the skin (to the way it looked before you had acne) is often not possible, but scar treatment does usually improve the appearance of your skin.

Dr Robin Stones, medical director for the North of England, at Court House Clinics, gives a brief explanation of scar treatments that are currently available:

Laser resurfacing

Traditional laser resurfacing has been the mainstay in the past. It involves stripping off the surface layers of skin, leaving a large surface area wound which, when it heals, leaves a smoother skin surface. Results are good but the disadvantages include the prolonged recovery time in comparison to other less aggressive treatments.

Dermabrasion

Dermabrasion works on a similar principle but instead of using a laser, a rotating mechanical device is used to remove the skin surface. This is very much a blunt instrument without the precise action of a laser beam, but carries all the same risks and is used relatively infrequently these days.

Fractional laser resurfacing

Fractional laser resurfacing is newer technology. A laser beam is fractionated into small dots (or pixels) in the same way as a TV screen or digital camera. The laser beam produces a dotted pattern on the skin. Each dot of laser energy penetrates the skin in a pixelated pattern producing micro-injuries, each dot surrounded by an area of normal skin. The injuries stimulate a wound healing reaction which generates new collagen, remodels damaged collagen and scar tissue, improving the appearance of the skin.

Dermaroller

Dermaroller is a rotating cylinder covered in tiny metal spikes which is rolled over the skin surface repeatedly to produce lots of tiny mechanical injuries, similar to the effect of a fractional laser. This stimulates a wound healing reaction in the same way. Usually three to five treatments are needed but the procedure and recovery time is less than 24 hours. The procedure is very well tolerated under topical anaesthesia. It can be supplemented by a roller with much smaller prongs designed for home use by the client.

Vavelta

Vavelta is the latest high tech treatment for some types of acne scarring. It is a cellular therapy using human dermal fibroblast cells from a donor source. Treatment involves the injection of living human skin repair cells into the affected area of the skin. The whole process can take weeks or even months.

LED light therapy

LED light therapy like Omnilux red and infra red light can help to reduce redness associated with scarring and also help to stimulate the skin's repair mechanisms. It combines well with more invasive procedures such as fractional laser resurfacing and Dermaroller.

Punch excision

Punch excision of deeply pitted ice pick scars involves using a circular punch (a device like a small apple corer) to remove individual deep scars. The skin edges are then stitched together to produce a level surface in place of the deep scar.

'There are many different treatments available now for acne scars including chemical peels and laser and dermabrasion treatments.'

Summing Up

- Everyone reacts to their condition differently. If you find that you are feeling depressed because of your acne, be sure to speak to someone you trust, like your GP or a family member.

- Maintaining a positive attitude is key to the treatment of your acne. Remember the three factors, acknowledgement, acceptance and action, to keep on top of emotional health and motivation.

- Physical scars can appear after acne has cleared but there are some effective treatments available to help with these. Speak to your GP or seek out a professional in this field to discuss your options.

Chapter Seven

Skin Care

Everyone should look after their skin on a daily basis, especially acne sufferers. It will help your skin look healthy and improve how you feel as a person. Even if you are taking medication for your acne, you can still implement a good skin care regime – this will only serve to complement the effects of the treatment.

The choices

Acne sufferers have to be extremely diligent when selecting skin care products. The type of skin care products that you use when you have acne can make a difference in how well your skin improves. In most cases, good skin care products will complement any medical treatment you will have undertaken.

The skin care market is a huge industry. People spend large amounts of money every year on skin care products. With the power of advertising we are often led to believe that one product might be better than another, but this is simply not the case. There is no brand that is better than another. However, there are some products available that address the issues most acne sufferers encounter in their battle against acne.

If you step inside any pharmacy, chemist or shop, you will encounter a large selection of acne skin care products. These include cleansers, toners, moisturisers, creams, gels and cosmetics.

Cleansers

Cleansers are the most popular acne skin care products. They are normally used to remove sweat, oil, dirt and make-up from the surface of your skin. This makes it easier for other acne treatments to be absorbed.

'Even if you are taking medication for your acne, you can still implement a good skin care regime – this will only serve to complement the effects of the treatment.'

Toners

Toners or astringents that are formulated for acne-prone skin remove the excess surface oil that can cause breakouts. They can be used one to three times per day, although frequent use may cause redness or irritation in people with extremely sensitive skin. Try to avoid alcohol based toners as they tend to dry the skin out.

Moisturisers

Many people with acne are hesitant to use a facial moisturiser. However, using a light, non-greasy moisturiser formulated especially for your skin type will help to keep your skin hydrated while preventing future breakouts. Look for products that are oil free.

'Acne treatments that use herbal ingredients are often less likely to cause allergic reactions or irritate sensitive skin.'

Creams and gels

Acne fighting creams or gels typically contain a more concentrated version of the ingredients found in other acne skin care products. If it is a cream or gel designed to combat acne, it will most certainly contain benzoyl peroxide (see opposite for an overview of the ingredients found in skin care products, as well as chapter 4 for information on ingredients found in proper acne treatments). If you have more sensitive skin, you may wish to opt for a cream or gel which has herbal ingredients.

Cosmetics

Women who are troubled by blemishes often choose to purchase make-up for acne-prone skin (non-comedogenic). There are many cosmetics that are formulated especially for acne-prone skin and some brands even match your skin tone and colour to specific products such as foundations and concealer to ensure you get the best coverage and effect. You can wear make-up over prescription creams and lotions but make sure that it is oil free.

Mix and match

You can either mix and match products from a variety of different manufacturers or purchase a complete skin care system from one company. There is no set rule about using products all from one range or brand, however it is essential that you use the correct ingredients. Always ask the sales assistant if they know whether the products you are buying are suitable for acne-prone skin – don't be talked into buying products that do not contain suitable ingredients. If you are in doubt, don't buy!

Ingredients

It is advised that you consult your GP before you start using any skin care products.

Although there are many different types of acne skin care products, most use the same active ingredients. Therefore, it's important to read labels carefully. Using several different products with the same active ingredients will increase the risk of irritation, possibly leading to additional skin problems. The ingredients found in specialist skin care products that you can buy in a shop are generally the same as those in treatments prescribed to you by your GP. However, skin care products are not used solely to combat acne, it is important for you to buy products designed to be used by acne sufferers.

Benzoyl peroxide

Benzoyl peroxide helps develop a clearer complexion by destroying acne-causing bacteria. It is an antiseptic and oxidising agent that can be found in a variety of concentrations. Common side effects can include dryness, itching and mild skin irritation.

Acne skin care products with benzoyl peroxide must be used for several weeks before you begin to see results.

Salicylic acid

If you have mild acne, acne skin care products containing salicylic acid can unclog pores to treat current pimples and prevent future breakouts. However, products with salicylic acid do not have any effect on sebum production or acne-causing bacteria.

For maximum effectiveness, products with salicylic acid must be used on a regular basis. Unfortunately, some acne sufferers experience skin irritation with frequent use of these products.

Herbal ingredients

If you're interested in natural skin care products, you'll be pleased to learn there are many acne treatments that use herbal ingredients to promote a clearer complexion.

Acne treatments that use herbal ingredients are often less likely to cause allergic reactions or irritate sensitive skin.

Essential skin care tips

- Implement a skin care routine which is as simple as possible. Keeping things simple will mean you are more likely to stick with a routine than get bored with it and give up.

- Remember that expensive skin care products are not always the best – they just look more appealing.

- Try to look for oil free or non-comedogenic products that will not clog your pores.

- Products aimed at oily skin types will help reduce surface oil and help keep the skin balanced.

- Be sure to thoroughly remove make-up at night.

- When you select your skin care products, be sure to explain your skin condition to the counter assistant and also mention any treatments that you are using.

Need2Know

- Beware of any claims made by counter or store assistants who suggest that your acne will go away if you use their products. Any such claims are not true and your acne will not go away with simple skin care products.

- Take the opportunity to test various products or book a makeover to see if you are happy with the results. Leave the products on your skin for a few hours and decide whether you think there is an improvement.

- Use balanced soap or soap free cleansers with a pH 5.5 balance. This will prevent natural oils being stripped away.

- Use an exfoliation product at least once a week. Exfoliating products are helpful because they help keep the skin free from a build-up of dead skin cells.

- If you do visit a beauty salon, be aware that few beauty therapists are trained to deal with acne. Explain your condition before you have any facial treatments or buy any skin care products.

- Continue to use a sunscreen but go for a light one that is non-comedogenic. Give yourself some time in between applying your acne treatment and sunscreen.

'Carry out as much research as you can before purchasing skin care products. If in doubt, ask your GP for advice before buying any.'

Summing Up

- A skin care regime using the right ingredients can complement any medical treatment you may receive for acne.

- Ensure you only purchase skin care products aimed at acne-prone skin. Check the label of the product carefully and always ask if it is suitable for acne sufferers.

- Carry out as much research as you can before purchasing skin care products. If in doubt, ask your GP for advice before buying any.

Chapter Eight

Expert Advice

Several experts have been brought together to answer many of the common questions and concerns acne sufferers have. For more accurate guidance, you can contact the experts in this section by using their details in the help list.

Meet the experts

Professor Laurence Kirwan MD FRCS was born in Britain and trained in aesthetic plastic surgery in the USA. He is now an international pioneering surgeon, practising in Harley Street, London, and in New York and Connecticut, USA.

Dr Sandeep Cliff is a leading consultant dermatologist and laser surgeon at Spire Gatwick Park Hospital. Having specialised in dermatology for over 15 years, Dr Cliff is a member of the British Association of Dermatologists as well as being an honorary senior lecturer at St George's Medical School in London.

Dr Robin Stones is the medical director of the Court House Clinic for the North of England. Dr Stones has a medical degree and he holds the Diploma in Dermatology from the Royal College of Physicians and Surgeons of Glasgow.

Jan Birch is managing director of The Blemish Clinic. Jan has over 20 years of experience in nursing and clinical research in photobiology and dermatology. She specialises in the use of photodynamic therapy for the treatment of skin cancers and cosmetic dermatology

Shaf Khan is a leading naturopathic herbalist born in the Midlands. He is a full practitioner member of the Association of Master Herbalists and works from three clinics in the Midlands. He is the founder of Shifa Herbs Naturopathic Health Consultancy. He is also the director of studies for the College of Naturopathic Medicine (Birmingham).

Dr Debra Luftman is a US board-certified dermatologist with a busy private practice in Beverly Hills. Dr Luftman is a leading expert on numerous anti-ageing treatments and constantly researches the latest technologies. She teaches general dermatology and skin surgery at the University of California, Los Angeles.

Q. I've started getting acne spots. How long do they last?

A. An acne breakout can last for months or even years. You should control breakouts with topical astringent antibiotics and oral antibiotics. You should visit your GP in the first instance to get you started on the right treatment.
(Professor Laurence Kirwan)

Q. My forehead is all spotty but I don't have acne anywhere else. Why is this?

A. It is possible for acne to just be localised to the forehead. The other possibility is a form of acne called pomade acne – this is seen in women and men who use oils in their hair which then spread to their foreheads, block the pores and lead to acne. This is best treated by encouraging the avoidance of these products.
(Dr Sandeep Cliff)

Q. Is it true that dabbing toothpaste on a spot can help it clear up?

A. Toothpaste is an irritant, so it's probably not a good idea to use it. It possibly has a drying effect on the skin. The idea that putting it on your skin will clear up spots is nothing but a myth.
(Jan Birch)

Q. I have just started taking antibiotics. How long will it be before I can expect to notice an improvement?

A. Antibiotics can start to work within 24-48 hours. Other treatments such as topical or oral vitamin A may take several weeks. Patience is the key to successful treatment.
(Professor Laurence Kirwan)

Q. I want to use a facial wash. Which is the best one?

A. The best face wash is one that exfoliates naturally. Neutrogena for people with acne is a good product.
(Dr Debra Luftman)

Q. How can I reduce the appearance of my acne scars?

A. Historically there were very limited options for treatment of established acne scarring, but in recent years a number of new treatments have become available. It is important that an acne patient understands that scarred skin will not become perfectly smooth but that the scarring will be less prominent and the appearance much improved.
(Dr Robin Stones)

Q. I'd quite like to see a homeopath for my acne. Is it very expensive?

A. Homeopathy is an energetic healing therapy which uses extreme dilution of substances. This may be administered by way of carrier pills or water drops. The assessment is based on a consultation analysing various aggravating factors. The costs can range depending on the practitioner. Some GPs are trained in homeopathy and therefore can prescribe through the NHS to about £90. However, this is dependent on the clinic locality and set up. Most registered homeopaths charge around £65 for an initial consultation.
(Shaf Khan)

'Patience is the key to successful treatment.'
Professor Laurence Kirwan.

Q. Can I still use sunscreen even though I have acne?

A. You should especially use sunscreen if you have acne. Acne causes inflammation and if exposed to sun it can cause pigmentation (darkening of the skin) and scarring. Sunscreen can help prevent this. Sunscreens with zinc and titanium are anti-bacterial.
(Dr Debra Luftman)

Q. My GP has suggested that I go and see a psychologist. What good will that be? I don't want to talk about my acne, I just want it to get better.

A. If you are anxious, stress can aggravate acne since hormones can control the function of the sebaceous glands. However, more specific medications are usually more beneficial. Seeing a psychologist can help you manage other factors which are important to acne sufferers, so don't write off the idea, it could help.
(Professor Laurence Kirwan)

Q. I am 29 and have just started to get spots. Is this the same as teenage acne?

A. Yes – it may be what is known as late-onset acne. Another possibility is acne rosacea [see page 29] – although different in many respects, it often resembles acne but is associated with flushing and broken blood vessels on the face. It can be made worse by sunlight. It's better to have a visual examination to determine what types of spots you have and a GP or a dermatologist can do this for you.
(Dr Sandeep Cliff)

'Alternative therapies are usually natural and therefore the chance of ill reaction is very remote.'
Shaf Khan.

Q. I have read that complementary medicine and alternative treatments can be dangerous and unsuccessful, so I am sceptical. However, I'm also afraid of taking lots of medicines.

A. Complementary medicine and alternative treatments can be very effective and powerful for many ailments, as some have been used for thousands of years. As with most treatments, there are risks. However, these alternative therapies are usually natural and therefore the chance of ill reaction is very remote. A professionally trained practitioner should be sought as they will endeavour to ascertain the appropriate treatment based on the consultation. Also the correct dosage instruction and advice would be given. A recommended and/or reputable practitioner is often your best option.
(Shaf Khan)

Q. The doctor has prescribed Dianette for my acne, but I am only 15 and my mum will get really upset if she thinks I am on the pill. Why am I taking a contraceptive?

A. Anti-androgen treatment is used as an alternative to antibiotics to treat problem skin. Dianette is one of these hormone treatments which often helps with moderate to severe acne. However, patients on this pill need to be closely monitored as it can damage the liver if used for long periods of time. You should explain to your mother what you are taking, and possibly ask your GP to explain to her why you are taking the medication. Maybe this way she will feel more at ease, and so will you.
(Jan Birch)

Q. What types of treatment are available for acne?

A. The treatment of acne must be directed at the type of spots you have. If the main problem is comedones, a benzoyl peroxide is beneficial. If the spots are mainly pustules then an antibiotic is of use. Treatment can be either oral or topical. If there are painful cysts and lumps then a more aggressive intervention such as isotretinoin may help. Determining the type of spots present on your skin, as well as the severity of the acne, is the first step in getting the right treatment for you.
(Dr Sandeep Cliff)

Q. What shall I tell my GP if I think I have acne?

A. It is very important to go to see your GP if you suffer with acne because it is a condition which can scar. You should go to your GP if you are not happy with your skin after trying acne products from your chemist, especially if your spots interfere with your enjoyment of life. If your spots are large and painful or scarring is beginning to form, explain this to your GP thoroughly.
(Jan Birch)

Q. What is the best way of covering my acne scars?

A. Minor scarring can be covered with light mineral make-up, and redness can be reduced by using a concealer with green tints. More significant redness can be concealed with professional camouflage make-up which has a natural

appearance and can be matched to individual skin colours. Depressed scars are impossible to cover and make-up will often collect in them, giving an unnatural appearance. This type of scarring is better treated with a medical procedure [see chapter 6].
(Dr Robin Stones)

Q. What is the best skin care routine?

A. The best skin care routine is one that follows the philosophy of KIS: keep it simple. You only need three products: an exfoliator, a sunscreen and a therapeutic night cream (often a retinol product) which treats acne and aging.
(Dr Debra Luftman)

Q. What is a comedone?

A. A comedone is a whitehead or blackhead produced by plugged pores.
(Dr Sandeep Cliff)

Q. Can spots be squeezed?

A. Try to resist the temptation to squeeze spots because this can force the contents of it deeper into the skin, making it look worse. However, if it's impossible to resist temptation (and only if the spot is yellow), follow these tips: wash your hands. Gently pull the skin around the spot apart to see if this allows it to burst. Avoid squeezing too hard as this could damage your skin. Once the yellow top has gone, stop squeezing. Clean with a moistened tissue.
(Jan Birch)

Q. Why is something called non-comedogenic? What exactly does this mean?

A. Non-comedogenic is the term used to describe something that does not block pores in the skin.
(Dr Debra Luftman)

Q. Is there a cure for acne?

A. There is no 100% cure for acne. However, there is a good chance of clinical success if the correct treatment is given to address the problem and the patient adheres religiously to the regime prescribed.
(Dr Sandeep Cliff)

Q. My friend had some very cold spray treatment for her raised scars. What was this?

A. The cold spray would be a treatment called 'cryotherapy' using liquid nitrogen or another cryogen. Liquid nitrogen is at a temperature of -196°C and literally freezes living tissue into ice. This has a local destructive effect, a bit like a controlled frostbite. The amount of tissue destroyed depends on the depth and duration of the freeze. It can be used to flatten off raised scars but is not suitable for depressed (hollow) scars. Treatment can be painful and healing may take one to two weeks. This treatment is commonly used in dermatological practice to treat warts, age spots and some skin cancers.
(Dr Robin Stones)

Q. I read in a magazine that isotretinoin (Roaccutane) can cure acne. Is it really that good?

A. Roaccutane, although a very effective treatment, is not the miracle cure it was once thought to be. It helps a lot of acne and is very effective, but up to 30% may relapse requiring a second course of treatment. Some do not respond at all.
(Dr Sandeep Cliff)

Q. If I am pregnant, do I have to stop my acne treatment?

A. If you become pregnant you can use a topical treatment. If your acne persists, it is not advisable to use systemic medication.
(Jan Birch)

'If you have any questions, doubts or issues regarding acne, it is always advisable to contact a professional expert such as your GP or a dermatologist.'

Q. I have heard that tea tree oil is good for spots. What's the best way of applying it?

A. You can apply tea tree oil directly to your spots but only if it's in a diluted form. Undiluted tea tree oil can cause irritation, itching or burning. Used correctly, the antibacterial action of the oil can decrease inflammation on the area it has been applied. You should consult a registered herbalist for more information.
(Shaf Khan)

Summing Up

- If you have any questions, doubts or issues regarding acne, it is always advisable to contact a professional expert such as your GP or a dermatologist.

- Make sure that any other practitioner you consult is a qualified professional and registered with a bona fide association.

- There are lots of support groups and associations also available that can help you with many questions. See the help list for details.

Chapter Nine

Case Studies

My experience of late-onset acne – Ms L Moss

'I had my first acne breakout at 20 years of age. I was very shocked as I had perfect skin as a teenager. To develop acne at 20 was really upsetting. I hadn't changed my diet, skin care products or make-up, so it was hard to understand why I suddenly had spots all over my face.

'I covered the spots up with really thick make-up as I was really embarrassed to have acne at my age. I generally felt very self-conscious and unattractive. Finally, I consulted my GP and she was really useful. She suggested that I start using a topical treatment called Quinoderm. After a period of time, this failed to work, so she put me on a course of treatment called Dianette. This also failed to work, so she referred me to a dermatologist.

'The dermatologist prescribed me an antiobiotic called tetracycline which cleared my acne in less than four weeks. However, as a side effect, the medication caused me to have a severe reaction to sunlight, so I had to stop taking it after three months.

'I read various books on the subject, but being an adult with acne made me feel somewhat isolated – spots are usually associated with teenagers!

'After reading an article in a newspaper, I tried a collection of skin care products called the Sher System. Although the products were expensive, they worked really well and left my skin wonderfully clear. They even helped to get rid of the blackheads I'd had since I was 12.

'To develop acne at 20 was really upsetting. I hadn't changed my diet, skin care products or make-up, so it was hard to understand why I suddenly had spots all over my face.'

Ms L. Moss.

'My advice to anyone suffering from acne is, firstly, don't blame yourself. Take the time to find a treatment that works for you. Whether that treatment is topical, oral, acupuncture or infrared light, it's important to find something that works in the long term and fits in with your lifestyle.

'I suffered from moderate acne which has gradually reduced. I have now had clear skin for the past 18 months.'

My experience of male adolescent acne – Mr S Matthews

'I'm 19 now but I've had acne since I was 17. It first started off with a few spots but they gradually increased in quantity, causing me to become quite self-conscious. My spots were inflamed and I noticed that I had blackheads as well as whiteheads. I washed my skin a lot and cleaned it well, so I was really confused as to why I kept developing spots.

'I visited my GP as I was worried that the problem would keep getting worse. He was really useful. He asked me questions about the spots, how long I had had them, how they started and what my diet and lifestyle was like. He made me feel really reassured. Then he carried out an inspection of my face, back and neck, and he diagnosed me with moderate acne. I was prescribed a topical cream which he explained contained peroxide, and also some antibiotic tablets called tetracycline. He told me to make a follow-up appointment in six weeks. I had to follow his instructions very carefully which I sometimes found hard as I was out with friends and didn't really have enough time to keep putting cream on.

'Nothing happened for about three and a half weeks but then I noticed a slight improvement. This really gave me a boost as I was beginning to get a bit upset as I thought the creams wouldn't work or that I was doing something wrong. By six weeks there was a definite improvement and I was feeling more positive by the time I went for my follow-up appointment. During the appointment, my GP told me to keep using the cream as it would continue to manage the spots.

'Sometimes I have a bad breakout (maybe once or twice a year) and my GP prescribes a topical retinoid which usually works. The acne is getting better and it is not as severe as it was two years ago.

'I look after my skin and try not to let the spots get me down (when I have them). I sometimes feel self-conscious but just try to get on with life as the acne will go away one day.'

My experience of male adolescent acne – Mr J Armstrong

'I started suffering from acne when I was 16. I'm now 19, so it took me three years before I found a successful solution for it.

'I visited my GP and after being diagnosed with severe acne, he prescribed me with antibiotics and creams. I waited patiently for them to get to work but nothing seemed to make the acne better. The spots were always inflamed and painful, and some were large and filled with pus. The acne really began to get me down. Within just one year I had tried so many different treatments and nothing seemed to work.

'Upon my last visit to the GP, I told him I was feeling quite depressed and would not go out as nothing would make my acne better. It was at this point that he decided to refer me to a dermatologist. The dermatologist also tried some treatments but, again, they did not work. Six months later, the acne was still there.

'At this point the dermatologist told me that Roaccutane was my last resort. I had to sign a consent form which explained the side effects of the medication. I started the course of Roaccutane and was on two pills a day. I had extremely dry lips and wore Chapstick all the time. I also had to have a blood test every two weeks. After four months I started to notice a significant difference in my skin – the spots had begun to disppear.

'When taking Roaccutane the spots do get worse initially, so you have to be prepared, be strong and remember that there will eventually be light at the end of the tunnel.'

My experience of female adolescent acne – Miss S Daikin

'I am 15 years old and have acne. I mostly have blackheads and a few red inflamed spots. I had heard a lot of people talking about a product which claimed to cure acne and after watching a TV programme about it, I decided to buy it off the Internet. I had read a lot about acne online and, judging by the look of my spots, I guessed I had mild to moderate acne.

'I read that this product I was going to buy contained benzoyl peroxide. I wasn't really sure what this meant but I knew it was one of the ingredients in a lot of acne products. The treatment I bought was really famous for being used by celebrities, so I was really excited to start using it.

'Within the first few days of use my blackheads got better and my skin felt a lot cleaner. However, I noticed that the towels I was using on my face started to bleach and looked discoloured. I started to get a bit worried about the strength of the treatment but carried on using it as I was convinced that it was really working.

'However, after two weeks my skin started to get really dry and sore. It even started to ache and flake off. My mum got worried about me and told me to see my GP. He told me that it is never a good idea to self-diagnose acne and that buying products from the Internet is not advised. He examined my skin and said that I did have mild acne and gave me a topical cream. He said that the cream contained benzoyl peroxide too but in the correct dosage for my type of acne.

'Now my spots are getting better. I am due to see my GP again in two weeks for a follow-up appointment. I am really scared by the fact that I could have ruined my skin by trying to find my own cure. I won't buy any more products from the Internet unless my GP says that it is okay to do so.'

> 'I won't buy any more products from the Internet unless my GP says that it is okay to do so.'
>
> Miss S Daikin.

My experience of adult acne – Ms D Schull

'I recently suffered a severe episode of acne during my mid-20s. It really blew my confidence and made me feel ugly, especially first thing in the morning and last thing at night. I had never had acne before and was extremely embarrassed. I didn't want to admit to myself that it was acne and just kept thinking "how can this be happening to me?" I was in denial despite many of my friends saying that the spots looked like acne.

'I covered myself up with foundation which only seemed to aggravate the problem, but I felt like I couldn't leave the house unless I had all my make-up on. It was like a shield of confidence and without it I felt vulnerable and exposed. In hindsight, all this make-up probably made my acne worse.

'After my dad insisted, I went to see a GP and a dermatologist. My dad said that if I didn't go and see someone, the problem was likely to get worse and I wouldn't feel any better. I was prescribed Dianette and topical creams and after about 12 weeks my skin started to improve (as did my confidence!). My treatment lasted a total of seven months before my acne cleared completely.

'My advice to any acne sufferer would be go and see your GP as soon as your spots start to become unmanageable. Try not to pick or squeeze spots as it can scar.'

'I felt like I couldn't leave the house unless I had all my make-up on.'

Ms D Schull.

Help List

Featured professional experts

Jan Birch, RGN, DipN, BSc (Hons), MSc, RICR, MBAS

The Blemish Clinic,113 Long Street, Middleton, Manchester, M24 6DL
Tel: 08000 852 309
jan.birch@blemishclinic.co.uk
www.blemishclinic.co.uk
Jan Birch is managing director of The Blemish Clinic and has over 20 years of
experience in nursing and clinical research in photobiology and dermatology.

Dr Sandeep H Cliff, FRCP BSc

Spire Gatwick Park Hospital, Povey Cross Road, Horley, Surrey, RH6 0BB
Tel: 01293 778968
sandeepcliff@hotmail.com
www.spirehealthcare.com
Dr Sandeep Cliff is a consultant dermatologist and laser surgeon at Spire
Gatwick Park Hospital.

Shaf Khan ND, Dip Herb Med

info@shifaherbs.com
www.shifaherbs.com
Shaf Khan is a leading naturopathic herbalist based in the West Midlands.

Professor Laurence Kirwan, MD FRCS

56 Harley Street, London, W1G 9QA
Tel: 020 7637 4455
www.cosmeticplasticsurgery.uk.com
Professor Kirwan is an international plastic surgeon, practising in Harley Street,
London, and in New York and Connecticut, USA.

Dr Debra Luftman MD

www.drluftman.com
www.thebeautyprescription.com
Dr Debra Luftman is a US board-certified dermatologist with a busy private practice in Beverly Hills.

Dr Robin Stones

Tel: 0845 555 5050
www.courthouseclinics.com
Dr Robin Stones is a cosmetic doctor and is also the Court House Clinic medical director for the North of England.

Organisations

British Association of Aesthetic Plastic Surgeons

Royal College of Surgeons, 35-43 Lincoln's Inn Fields, London, WC2A 3PE
Tel: 020 7430 1840 (office)
www.baaps.org.uk
The aim of BAAPS is to improve cosmetic surgery training through annual meetings, where surgeons present scientific papers and teach their skills to others. BAAPS is also creating links with the European Association of Societies of Aesthetic Plastic Surgeons (EASAPS) as well as the International Society of Aesthetic Plastic Surgery (ISAPS). In doing so, BAAPS is helping to raise the standards of aesthetic/cosmetic surgery around the world. On the website, you can find out about plastic surgery and also use the 'find a surgeon' tool.

British Association of Dermatologists

Willan House, 4 Fitzroy Square, London, W1T 5HQ
Tel: 0207 383 0266
admin@bad.org.uk
www.bad.org.uk
BAD preserves books relating to the history of dermatology. It also organises an annual conference and has commissioned a regional history of

dermatology. It is a professional organisation for all dermatologists in the UK. They aim to support patients and improve practice standards. The website includes general information on skin, dermatology and various skin diseases.

British Association of Skin Camouflage

PO Box 3671, Chester, CH1 9QH
Tel: 01254 703107 (10am-4pm, Monday to Friday)
info@skin-camouflage.net
www.skin-camouflage.net
BASC is internationally recognised as the leading provider of professional training in the specialist area of skin camouflage. On the website, you can find out about skin camouflage, who it is suitable for and what products are used.

British Complementary Medicine Association

PO Box 5122, Bournemouth, BH8 0WG
Tel: 0845 345 5977
www.bcma.co.uk
The BCMA is an independent body which holds an international register of insured and qualified holistic therapists. You can use the website to see if there is a clinic located near you which delivers alternative therapies.

Changing Faces

The Squire Centre, 33-37 University Street, London, WC1E 6JN
Tel: 0845 4500 275
info@changingfaces.org.uk
www.changingfaces.org.uk
Changing Faces is the UK's leading charity which supports and represents individuals who live with disfigurement. It provides personal support for children and adults and also works with the government and media to campaign for social change.

Institute for Complementary and Natural Medicine

ICNM, Can-Mezzanine, 32-36 Loman Street, London, SE1 0EH
Tel: 0207 922 7980
www.i-c-m.org.uk

The ICNM is a registered charity which provides the public with information on complementary and natural medicine. It aims to treat patients in all aspects of the body, mind and spirit, while using means of minimal intervention.

MIND

England

15-19 Broadway, London, E15 4BQ

Tel: 020 8519 2122

Wales

3rd Floor, Quebec House, Castlebridge, 5-19 Cowbridge Road East, Cardiff, CF11 9AB

Tel: 029 2039 5123

contact@mind.org.uk

www.mind.org.uk

MIND is the leading mental health charity for England and Wales involved in campaigning, providing information to the public and supporting those who live with mental distress.

Netdoctor

www.netdoctor.co.uk

Use this website to find out about many medical conditions and get advice from real health professionals.

NHS Choices

www.nhs.uk

You can use this website to find information on any health-related topics. There is a symptom checker tool and explanations for hundreds of medical conditions.

NHS Direct (Health Information Service)

Tel: 0845 4647

www.nhsdirect.nhs.uk

NHS Direct is available 24 hours a day, 365 days a year. It offers out-of-hours support for GPs and dental services, telephone support for patients with long-term conditions, pre and post-operative support for patients, 24-hour response to health scares and remote clinics via telephone.

Primary Care Dermatology Society

2nd Floor, Titan Court, 3 Bishop Square, Hatfield, AL10 9NA
Tel: 01707 226024
www.pcds.org.uk
The PCDS organises educational conferences and a quarterly bulletin and forums which seek to redress the under provision of dermatology education in primary care.

Skin Care Campaign

Hill House, High Gate Hill, London, N19 5NA
Tel: 07810564913
alangford@skincarecampaign.org
www.skincarecampaign.org
The Skin Care Campaign is a subsidiary of the National Eczema Society, representing the interests of people in the UK with skin diseases.

Skinship

Plascow Cottage, Kirkgunzeon, Dumfries, DG2 8JT
Tel: 01387 760 567
www.ukselfhelp.info/skinship
Skinship manages calls from people around the UK who are dealing with skin problems.

Skin Treatment and Research Trust (START)

Chelsea and Westminster Hospital, 369 Fulham Road, London, SW10 9NH
Tel: 020 8746 8174
gailstart@email.com
START is dedicated to supporting doctors with an interest in dermatology and related research projects.

Recommended skin care brands

Clearasil

www.clearasil.co.uk
Long-established quality skin care products with good ingredients, formulated for acne-prone skin.

Clinique

www.clinique.co.uk
Clinique's anti-blemish solutions are packed with highly effective ingredients and all come in gentle, comfortable formulas.

Cover FX Cosmetics

www.coverfx.com
Cosmetics developed in a dermatology clinic designed to cover up flaws in the skin such as acne and scars.

Dermalogica

www.dermalogica.com/uk
Products with a reputation for delivering good results through education and innovation, not through advertising, frilly packaging or miracle cures.

Dr Hauschka

www.drhauschka.co.uk
All Dr Hauschka products carry the BDIH seal of 'Certified Natural Cosmetics' and are made from natural ingredients.

Environ

www.vitaminskincare.eu
Environ Skin Care was founded by South African cosmetic surgeon Dr Des Fernandes. The products are highly effective and can be used for the protection and maintenance of smooth, even toned and healthy skin.

Jane Iredale Cosmetics

www.janeiredaleuk.eu
Quality cosmetics formulated with specific ingredients for acne-prone skin.

Jan Marini

www.janmarini.com
Jan Marini is a respected national skin care authority that has dedicated more than three decades to researching and developing new and innovative skin care technologies that deliver real results.

Oxy

www.oxy.co.uk
A good selection of skin care products formulated for acne-prone skin.

Priori AHA Skin Care

www.cosmestore.co.uk
Formulated by skin care pioneers, Priori AHA Skin Care incorporates the latest research advancements combined with state-of-the-art ingredients.

Book List

100 Questions and Answers About Acne (Class Health)
by Doris M Day, Jones and Bartlett Publishers, USA, 2004.

Acne: Answers At Your Fingertips
by Dr Tim Mitchell and Alison Dudley, Class Publishing, London, 2002.

Acne for Dummies
by Herbert P Goodheart MD, John Wiley & Sons, USA, 2006.

The Acne-Free Diet Plan: 30 Days to Clearer Skin
by Dean R Goodless MD, Lulu.com, USA, 2005.

Breaking Out: A Woman's Guide to Coping with Acne at Any Age
by Lydia Preston, Fireside, USA, 2004.

The Clear Skin Diet: How to Defeat Acne and Enjoy Healthy Skin
by Alan C Logan, Cumberland House Publishing, USA, 2007.

Clear Skin: Organic Action Plan for Acne
by Julie Gabriel, iUniverse.com, USA, 2007.

The Clear Skin Prescription
by Nicholas Perricone, Harper Collins, London, 2004.

The Good Skin Doctor: A Dermatologist's Survival Guide to Acne
by Tony Chu and Anne Lovell, Thorsons, London, 1999.

The Pocket Guide to Acne
by Amrit Darvay and Anthony Chu, Blackwell Publishing, Oxford, 2000.

Solve Your Skincare Problems
by Natalie Savona and Patrick Holford, Piatkus Books, London, 2001.

Warts and All: Straight Talking Advice on Life's Embarrassing Problems
by Margaret Stean, Murdoch Books, London, 2007.

Glossary

Acne conglobata
A very severe type of acne in which nodules are connected to other nodules or acne lesions beneath the surface of the skin.

Acne mechanica
A form of acne that develops in response to heat, covered skin, constant pressure and/or repetitive friction against the skin.

Acne vulgaris
The medical term for common acne which is characterised by the presence of one or more of the following: blackheads, whiteheads, papules and pustules.

Androgenic
Referring to the hormones that stimulate the sebaceous glands to create sebum.

Androgens
Hormones that stimulate sebaceous glands in addition to other effects on the body. Present in both males and females, androgens are responsible for physical maturation in males and therefore occur in much higher levels in males. Males tend to have more severe acne than females.

Blackhead
A non-inflammatory acne lesion that is filled with excess oil and dead skin cells. Blackheads are also called open comedones because the surface of the skin remains open.

Closed comedone
A whitehead – a non-inflammatory comedone with a white centre.

Comedone
An acne lesion (plural: comedones).

Comedogenic
Likely to cause comedones.

Follicle
The tiny shaft in the skin through which a hair grows and sebum is excreted.

Fungistatic substance
A substance or product able to inhibit the growth and/or reproduction of at least some types of fungi.

Hormones
Chemical substances produced by the body that, depending on the hormone, govern many bodily processes. Certain hormones cause physical maturation during puberty. These are the ones implicated in acne.

Inflammatory
Meaning to cause inflammation. In acne, inflammatory is usually used to describe lesions that are inflamed by chemical reactions or bacteria in clogged follicles.

Isotretinoin
A systemic medication used to treat severe forms of acne. Due to potential birth defects, a woman must not take this medication while pregnant or breast feeding and must not become pregnant while taking it.

Keloid
A large raised scar that spreads beyond the size of the original wound.

Lipids
Oily substances that include things like fats, oils and waxes. Sebum is made up of lipids. A particular kind of lipid, free fatty acids are irritating to the skin.

Macule
A flat spot or patch of skin that is not the same colour as the surrounding skin.

Melanin
The substance that gives hair and skin its colour.

Microcomedone
The first stage of comedone formation – a comedone so small that it can be seen only with a microscope.

Nodulocystic acne
A severe form of acne that is characterised by numerous deep, inflamed bumps (nodules) and large, pus-filled lesions that resemble boils (cysts). The

nodules are tender when touched and feel firm. The severe inflammation can cause the acne to become very red or even purple. Scarring often results when the acne heals.

Non-comedogenic
Not likely to cause comedones.

Non-inflammatory
In acne, comedones that are not associated with redness in the skin.

Open comedone
A blackhead – a non-inflammatory comedone with a dark top and firmly packed contents.

Papule
An inflammatory comedone that resembles a small, red bump on the skin.

Papulopustular
A type of acne characterised by the presence of papules and pustules.

Post-inflammatory hyperpigmentation
Excessive skin darkening at places where the skin was inflamed.

Propionibacterium acnes (P acnes)
A normal resident on the skin, P acnes will multiply rapidly in clogged hair follicles where sebum is trapped.

Puberty
The time of life when a child begins the physical maturation process toward adulthood. Onset is usually in the early teens and is accompanied by a large increase in hormone production.

Pustule
An inflammatory comedone that resembles a whitehead with a ring of redness around it.

Retinoid
A natural or synthetic substance derived from vitamin A used to treat acne.

Sebaceous glands
Glands in the skin that produce an oily substance called sebum. These glands are the sites of acne lesions. Sebaceous glands are attached to hair follicles and are found mostly on the face, neck, back and chest.

Sebum

The oily substance produced by sebaceous glands.

Systemic therapy

Treatment that consists of taking medication internally, such as in pill form or by injection or infusion.

White blood cells

Components of the blood that help fight off infections.

Whitehead

An acne lesion that forms when oil and skin cells block the opening of a hair follicle. For this reason, whiteheads are called 'closed comedomes'.